Ghosts and Ghoulies

Thrillogy

Edited by Paul Collins and Meredith Costain

sundance
A Haights Cross Communications Company

Read all of the
 Titles

Fantasy/Horror

Dragon Tales

Ghosts and Ghoulies

Heroic Feats

Last Gasps

Tales from Beyond

Terrors of Nature

Science Fiction

Alien Invasions

Gadgets and Gizmos

It Came from the Lab . . .

Lost in Space

Techno Terror

Time Zones

 **sundance**

A Haights Cross Communications Company

Published by Sundance Publishing
P.O. Box 740, One Beeman Road, Northborough, MA 01532

Copyright in individual stories remains with the authors.

First published 1999 as Spinouts by
Addison Wesley Longman Australia Pty Limited
95 Coventry Street, South Melbourne 3205 Australia
Exclusive United States Distribution: Sundance Publishing

ISBN 0-7608-4836-X

Printed in China

Contents

The Test

The author
David Hill
talks about the story

"*The Test* began after I thought about how it's weird that we think all ghosts can do all sorts of supernatural things. Why shouldn't there be geeky ghosts, just like there are geeky humans? And then I invented Reg."

David Hill

The Test

A day after Chad and his mom reached the new town, they found an apartment. A day after they found the apartment, they found a school for Chad. A day after Chad started school, he found Lenny Heaps.

Actually, Lenny found Chad. He found him looking at the bulletin board, and he kicked Chad's bag halfway down the hall, sending pens and books flying. The day after that, Lenny rammed his meaty shoulder into Chad and sent him halfway down the hall.

Lenny sat behind Chad in assembly, grinding his knuckles into Chad's back. He threw Chad's library books on the roof. He lived just two streets away, so even as Chad walked home, he wasn't safe from Lenny's pushings and sneerings.

At home on Monday afternoon, Chad sat reading, trying to keep his mind off Lenny Heaps. His mom was due home in an hour. The pages of his book flipped over from a draft. Now he'd lost his place.

The pages turned faster. "Stop!" Chad snapped.

From somewhere in the room, a voice spoke. "You cannot stop me. I am The Great Darkness."

Black terror flooded through Chad. And then black terror became red rage. He'd had enough of being bullied. "Great Darkness, my eye! You're a Great Geek!"

Silence in the room. But Chad knew something was there. He kept his voice loud so it wouldn't tremble. "Come on! What are you?"

The voice spoke again from near the stove. "I'm a poltergeist. I haunt places. I throw things around and scare people."

"Well, you're a useless polterwhatsit, 'cause you don't scare me. Prove it, anyway. Go on — throw something."

Another silence. The skin on Chad's back prickled. Then his head jerked sideways. The voice had moved to the cabinet.

"All right." The poltergeist sounded nervous. "Prepare to be terrified."

A cup on the shelf moved slowly sideways, rolled back, then moved sideways again. After four starts, the cup reached the edge of the shelf. It teetered over the edge, then fell.

"Yes!" yelled the voice. The cup dropped a few feet, hit something invisible, and bounced sideways. "Aaarghh!" went the voice. "My knee!"

"You're the most useless poltergeist around," said Chad as he picked up the cup.

"You do it with no hands then!" complained the voice. "Think you're big and tough, do you?"

Chad thought of Lenny Heaps. "No," he said. "No, I don't."

On Wednesday, Chad rushed home, hurrying to keep ahead of Lenny. In two minutes, the pages of his book began to stir.

The voice came from the far end of the table this time. "I am The Great Darkness."

"I'm not gonna call you that. It sounds stupid. What's your real name?"

Chad leaped as the voice spoke from behind him. "Reginald."

"Hi, Reg. Listen, would you mind not wandering all around the place? It's a little scary!"

"Really?" The poltergeist sounded pleased. "Cool! Poltergeists are supposed to scare people. That's what The Lords of Fear look for when they test you. And my test's coming up soon."

Chad grunted. "Maybe The Lords of Fear can help me stop Lenny Heaps, the big ape!"

"Lenny who?" asked the voice from under the table. Chad explained.

"You've got to stand up to a guy like that." Reg's voice was halfway up a wall — he must be standing up. "Give it to him! Show him who's boss."

"Like you do?" Chad muttered to himself.

Two afternoons later, as Chad walked home from school, a shoulder rammed him from behind. He staggered, bounced off a telephone pole into a bush, then fell over the bush onto a lawn. "Who's a little ballet dancer?" sneered Lenny's voice.

Squeak!

"That's it," Chad decided. "Next time that Heaps creep picks on me, I'll . . . I'll — do something!"

Inside the apartment, he sat and stared in front of him. He jumped when a voice spoke above his head. "I am The Great Darkness."

"Hey, did I frighten you?" the voice asked. "Awesome! The Lords of Fear will be so impressed!"

"Shut up, Reg. I am frightened. But it's . . . "

"It's what?" the poltergeist's voice demanded. "That guy Benny Beeps? I told you — you've gotta stand up to him!"

"How would you know?" Chad said to himself. And anyway, he thought, how do I stand up to Lenny Heaps when I only reach up to his smelly armpits?

Chad heard the heavy footsteps behind him as he got near his apartment the next afternoon. He walked on, listening intently. He sensed Lenny lowering his shoulder for another meaty shove and darted sideways. The big boy tried to stop himself but went sprawling halfway across Chad's next-door neighbor's mailbox.

"I always knew you were junk mail!" Chad laughed and sprinted up the path to the apartment. Behind him, Lenny struggled to his feet.

In the apartment, yesterday's newspaper lay scattered across the table. "Hey, Reg!" Chad called. "You were right! I stood up to — "

The apartment door burst open behind Chad. Lenny Heaps stood in the doorway.

The beefy boy sneered. "Think you're smart, ya little creep? Well, I'm smarter. I've seen when your mother comes home. Not for an hour yet, huh? Enough time to teach you a few lessons."

Chad retreated around the kitchen table. Lenny grinned and kicked a chair away, sending it tumbling on its side. "Yeah, a few lessons," he repeated.

Chad stopped. He'd had enough. OK, he was gonna get his head ripped off, but he wasn't running any more. "You're the one who needs lessons, you ape."

"Big mouth for a little creep," Lenny sneered. "Think I'll . . ." Lenny's voice trailed away. The chair was rising up from the floor, all by itself.

A hollow voice spoke. "A few lessons. Yes, a few lessons."

Lenny's mouth shook. With a crash, the chair dropped to the floor again. "Think you're smart?" the voice growled. "Think you're smart?"

Lenny backed against the wall. Mumbling noises came from his mouth. His hands were up, as if trying to push something away.

Suddenly, the radio switched on. Music blared. Lenny screamed. And then the newspaper took off from the table. It soared into the air until the room seemed full of flying pages. They churned around Lenny's face. He screamed again. Arms over his head, he staggered for the door.

It slammed shut in front of him. Lenny clawed at the handle. "Not for an hour yet." The voice seemed deeper and more powerful with each sentence.

Lenny sank to his knees. "Let me go! Please!"

"I am The Great Darkness." The poltergeist's voice rolled like thunder.

Lenny shrieked. "Let me go! I'll do anything!"

Total silence. Then the thunder rolled again. "Go and never return. If you bother this boy again, The Great Darkness will seize you. Never return! Do you promise?"

"I promise! I'll never come here again!"

"Then go!" The door flew open, hitting Lenny on the nose. He plunged through the doorway, still whimpering. Sprinting footsteps faded down the drive.

Inside the apartment, there was another silence. Then the invisible voice spoke again. "Pretty cool, huh? The Lords of Fear should be satisfied with that."

"Awesome, Reg!" exclaimed Chad, picking up the chair and newspaper. "How did you do it? That was . . . that was out of this world."

"I surprised myself." The voice drifted down to the table. "But that guy was scaring you. That's supposed to be *my* job!"

Chad arrived home whistling the following afternoon. He'd seen Lenny Heaps just once at school. The beefy boy gave him a terrified look and hurried away.

He opened the door and grinned. A black notebook floated in the middle of the dining room. A black pen floated above it.

"Nice one, Reg."

But the voice that replied was different — slow and old. "The Great Darkness is elsewhere. I have come to record his deeds."

"Hey," said Chad. "Are you a Lord of Fear?"

"Correct. I am The Mighty Mazool. I understand a successful frightening happened here yesterday."

"Yeah!" Chad grinned. "Reg gave Lenny heaps of fright!"

The black pen scribbled. The Great Darkness Verdict: Very Satisfactory. "Thank you for your cooperation."

"So where is Reg? I mean The Great Darkness?" Chad asked.

"Promoted. He sends you his best wishes and hopes to drop in soon. Farewell, young mortal. Have a nice day." There was a shimmer of green light. Then the notebook and pen vanished.

As Chad sat down, he thought of what he'd just said to the Mighty Mazool. It wasn't quite true. Reg hadn't just given Lenny heaps of fright. He'd given Lenny Heaps heaps.

The Worst Thing
in the World

The author
Rosaleen Love
talks about the story

"When I was asked to write this story, I remembered one wild thing that happened to me. It really did freak me out. I went camping. One night, I saw the shadows move. But there wasn't a trace of wind. I didn't move all night."

Rosaleen Love

The Worst Thing in the World

Josh and Harvey were best friends. They often went camping together. Josh said to his mother, "I don't want to go without Harvey." That was how Harvey knew what happened when Josh went camping with his family. Harvey was there.

The story Harvey tells about what happened one night at Pinnacle Beach is a very strange story.

To start with, Pinnacle Beach is one weird place. Large stones stand upright on the sand. They look like thousands of soldiers marching down to the sea.

In the daytime, they are just big lumps of stone. At night, they cast long shadows. That first night, there was a full moon. All around the camp site, the stone pinnacles stood guard. They stood like a ring of soldiers around the campfire watching Josh and Harvey.

Harvey made the campfire just the way he liked it. Large hunks of wood turned to deep red coals. Harvey took a stick and broke the coals so the

sparks flew up and out. He sat dreaming, not noticing the stones. Not that time.

Suddenly, he heard noises like moans coming from the shadows.

That was the first time Josh disappeared.

Harvey wasn't scared, not the first time. He saw that Josh wasn't beside him, by the fire, and he figured Josh was hiding behind one of the pinnacles, tricking him.

Harvey crept into the dark and hid. He could feel the moon shining on his back. The moon pushed him with cold moon fingers. He pressed himself against the weathered stone. He heard more moans coming from behind other stones, like echoes.

"Uh-oh," Harvey told himself. "Now it's time for spooks." Except he didn't believe in spooks. He knew it was just a trick of the stones — echoes and sounds bouncing around in the dark. He darted from pinnacle to pinnacle, trying to find out where the noises were.

Then he saw Josh. He was standing quite still, looking at the moon.

Josh bellowed. He let out one wild yell.

Harvey was puzzled, and so was Josh when he calmed down. There seemed to be other voices out there in the dark, other sounds. And the pinnacles looked even more like rows of gravestones in the moonlight.

Josh was shaking. He was terrified. "I don't remember . . ." His voice trailed off.

Harvey picked up a stone and threw it at the shadows. "Gotcha!" he yelled.

"I don't remember," Josh mumbled again. "I was there." He pointed to the fire. "And then I was here. But I don't know how I got here!"

Harvey threw a rock at a shadow. He ran and shouted and laughed. He fought the shadows. He scared the darkness away . . . for the moment.

It wasn't like Josh to be scared. Josh was without fear. He was always the first to seek thrills.

Harvey didn't like it. Something wasn't right.

The next day Josh and Harvey got up early and went exploring. Harvey looked for wood for the fire.

He liked piling up the little sticks before the fire started. He liked watching the tiny flames flicker into life. Harvey got busy and didn't notice Josh had disappeared again, until he heard a yell. "Harvey! Quick! Come here!"

Harvey ran to the top of the sand hill and peered over the top. The surf pounded on the rocks below.

He saw a hand at the edge of a large slab of rock. The fingers beckoned to him.

Josh yelled, "Here!" There was a crack between two large slabs of rock. Josh was inside, with just his arm outside. Harvey squeezed through the crack.

The two boys were in a cave. It had rough stone walls, and the roof was open to the sky.

People had been here before. They had written their names on the walls. *Farrow. Pringle. Oates. 1824.*

Then there was the name of a ship. *HMS Shaw.*

There had been a shipwreck here a long time ago. Harvey kicked the rocks on the cave floor, looking for bones. He didn't find any.

Josh went along a dark passage further into the cave. Harvey didn't want to follow Josh. He wanted to get out. There was a sharp animal smell in the air.

Josh screamed and came running out. Large black shapes followed him, tumbling from the walls. The air heaved, black and alive. Bats! They were bats! They took off into the sky.

The two boys ran out and scrambled up the face of the cliff. They stood there, at the top of the cliff, panting. The bats flew in drooping circles in the sky until, stunned by the heat, they finally fell back into the cave.

Pinnacle Beach was a place with secrets. Harvey and Josh were scared. The pinnacles were down there, under the ground. Half in, half out of the cave walls, rooted in the sand. Those sailors had died in there. Harvey felt it in his bones.

Harvey didn't like the cave. He didn't like the beach. He didn't like the pinnacles. They went so deep into the ground. Perhaps they had been dropped from the sky. They'd hit the earth — pow, pow, pow — and stood up straight and tall.

They were planned that way. Their pattern, which looked like no pattern, was planned by someone. Or something. Maybe a spaceship had come to a place that reminded its passengers of home. Maybe they'd dropped stone messages. People send each other letters, thought Harvey. Perhaps spaceships send messages with stones. Spaceships had come and left their soldiers behind to watch over things.

That night Harvey was zipped up tight in his sleeping bag. He thought about Josh. Josh was good at everything. It wasn't like Josh to be scared. Josh was without fear. At least he acted that way. Harvey drifted off to sleep.

The next thing he knew, he was out in the moonlight. There was Josh. Josh didn't notice Harvey. Harvey didn't know what to do. Josh walked up the hill toward the cliff at the edge of the beach. His eyes were open, but he seemed asleep. Harvey ran after him. Wherever Josh went, Harvey followed.

Josh moved quickly and surely across the sand. Bats flew swiftly through the night sky. By day, the pinnacles were different from each other, each weathered in its own way. That night, there was something new. One of the pinnacles glowed in the dark. The light of the moon shone upon it and the space around it.

Josh was drawn like a moth to a flame.

Harvey saw the light and the spaces in between the stones. The light curled up in the dark, empty spaces, and the dark came out to greet Josh. The pinnacle stood strong and firm in the moonlight, casting no shadow. The shadows had gone somewhere else to gather their strength.

The moon stood high in the sky. The wind ruffled the sand. Then, from the edges of the light, the shadows came to get Josh. Josh walked into the spaces in between the stones. He walked into deep danger as a door opened into another world. Dark shapes swirled high in the air, then fell upon Josh. At the very last minute, they veered away from him. Again they swooped, and fell, and veered off.

And as they swooped, Harvey saw mouths in the shadows, and eyes, watching. He was powerless.

The shapes swooped and took off again, each time driving Josh a little bit closer to them. Harvey tried to move, but his feet wouldn't let him. Then Josh turned and ran away. He was running so fast he stumbled and fell over.

"Get up!" Harvey yelled. "Run!" Harvey tried to give Josh strength to stand and fight once more. But Josh was losing the fight. He grew weaker. He could twist and turn no more. His eyes were large and black and glowing.

The shadows seeped around the edges. Two sailors stepped out of the shadows — ghost sailors. Men who had been here before and died here long ago. Two men, Pringle and Farrow. They wafted over to Josh and lifted him easily. They weren't interested in Harvey. They weren't tuned in to his wavelength. It was Josh they were after. They moved off into the darkness.

The door to another world had opened. Then it had closed. The sailors went about their business. And their business, that night, was Josh.

Underneath the ground there is a city of pinnacles. They stare out from the stone, the sailors who had been here before, the wanderers, the lost ones.

They live in stone as once they lived in air. Their eyes are open, their ears hear, their bodies feel the cold.

One day wind and rain and waters rising from the sea will wear down the earth, and the forest of stone people will rise to the air. Josh will be among them.

Harvey tells this story and some people believe him. Others don't know what to think. All they know is that Josh has disappeared, and no one has found him yet.

It's a terrible thing, to be lost and never found. It's the worst thing in the world.

The
School
Fair

The author
Kaaron Warren
talks about the story

"When I was young, my grandfather got sunstroke because he wanted to sit outside and watch us play. The image of him sitting there, getting redder and redder, flashes into my mind every now and then, so I decided to write a story about it."

The School Fair

"You're the big fish in a little pond, here," Mrs. Luff said. "You must set an example for the younger children." It was a hot day. She wiped her underarms with a tissue and dropped it in the wastebasket.

"Yuck," I whispered to Susie. It was dangerous, sitting next to her. We always got the giggles at the stupidest things, and Mrs. Luff hated the giggles.

Susie giggled.

"Susie and Katie, maybe you'd like to be the first to volunteer for a booth at our school fair. How about the ghost house?"

I shuddered. Number one, the cool kids would kill us. The cool kids in sixth grade always run the ghost house.

Number two, I hate ghosts, even fake ones. I hate thinking about them or hearing about them. I get scared even reading fairy tales because they remind me of ghosts. Mom thinks it's because I thought I

saw a ghost when I was about four. I think it's because I *did* see a ghost.

I was out playing in the driveway. I had made a whole city there — a playground, a castle, a swimming pool, and a candy shop — the kind of city a four-year-old would call perfect. Then I looked up, and there was an old man on the steps. His face was bright red and sweaty. His hat was tilted back. He had no teeth.

I dropped the rock that was about to become a mountain, screamed, and ran inside. Even at that age, I knew you shouldn't talk to strangers.

"What's the matter?" Mom asked, holding me tightly.

"There's a man in the driveway." Mom ran to the window. There was no one there. We live on a long, flat street, and she looked both ways.

"He's gone now, honey," she said. She told me a few years ago, when I started to realize how scared I was of ghosts, that she didn't think the man had ever been there.

I hate ghosts.

"Well, Katie? Ghost house?" Mrs. Luff said.

"We could run the book sale," I said desperately.

"Book sale?" Susie said in disgust. It was the loser booth. I love books myself, and so does Susie.

So do most of the other kids, but you don't let the grown-ups know that.

"Good idea," said Mrs. Luff. The other kids were happy because they sure didn't want to run the book sale.

Later, we all planned the ghost house. Of course, everyone had to tell their favorite ghost story.

I hated it.

Matthew said, "Yeah, this time we went way down the beach. I was exploring in these caves with my little brother, and we saw all of these bones. They were really big, not like you get after eating a turkey, really big, like they were human bones. Anyway, I told my brother not to touch them, and we left and told Mom and Dad. They took us to

tell the police. The police asked if we'd moved anything, and we said no."

"That night my brother was snoring and keeping me awake, and I heard this scratching at the window. I thought it must be a bird or something, so I ignored it. Then I heard knocking. And we were on the second floor! I woke my brother up to hear it, too. He went to the window and opened it to look out, and this misty stuff came in. It was freezing. The mist turned into a man with only one arm. He said to us, 'Give me back my arm.' 'We haven't got it,' I said. But my brother said, 'I've got it.' He crawled under the bed and got one of the bones we saw in the cave. He gave it to the ghost. The ghost said, 'Never steal from anyone, or you will be punished.' And since then I never have."

"Thank you, Matthew," said Mrs. Luff. At least I think that's what she said. I had my fingers in my ears.

The day of the fair was beautiful and sunny. Of course, Mrs. Luff thought it was all because of her.

I was really looking forward to it. I'd helped the adults sort all of the books the night before, and I was planning to be the super salesperson and sell them all. "Have you read any Tolkien?" I'd say, holding out *The Hobbit* and *Lord of the Rings*.

"This one's got some good stuff in it," I'd say. I'd sell every book.

Huh. Great fantasy, Katie. *No one* came to the book sale while I was there.

Not one person.

They'd get close, then walk away. It was spooky.

Finally, Mr. King told me to take a break. He's the *nice* sixth-grade teacher. If I had him, I would love sixth grade.

I walked over to Susie and some of our friends, who were eating spring rolls. Susie looked a bit guilty because she was supposed to be helping, too. But I didn't say anything about that.

"No one's buying books today. It's weird," I said.

They all looked at each other, then over at the book table.

It was packed.

"I better go help," I said. I ran over. I didn't want to miss those sales.

As soon as I stood behind the table, everyone left.

Mr. King and I stared at each other.

"Take another break, Katie," he said. I slowly walked away.

I turned around. The booth was packed.

"I didn't realize I was so ugly," I said to Susie. I was close to tears, but Mrs. Luff's words kept coming back to me. "You must set an example for the younger children."

"It's not you, it's that old man, your grandfather or whoever," Susie said. "He's hanging around, scaring people off."

I stared at her. "One grandfather lives overseas, the other one's been dead since I was one," I said. "He died of sunstroke." I touched my hat. We're careful about the sun in my family.

I walked slowly back to my spot behind the book table and looked behind me. Then I screamed and stepped back, backing into the table of books and sending a few crashing to the ground.

"Katie!" Mr. King cried, grabbing at the books that were scattered on the ground.

I was speechless.

There was the ghost. He looked just the same as he did when I was four years old; sweaty, hat tilted back, red face. I couldn't get past him to run away.

"Katie! Stop banging the table!" Mr. King said. Without taking my eyes off the old man, I helped Mr. King restack the books.

"We probably should move the booth, anyway," Mr. King said. "It's too cold here in the shade. People keep shivering as they walk past. Let's move it over there into the sun."

The old man moved to stand under the tree that was shading us. I could get out. I felt his eyes burning through me, though.

We moved the booth. We started selling books. I kept turning around to see the old man, but he was gone.

Near the end of the fair, Mr. King took a break. I liked being on my own. I was selling the last of the Tolkien to Susie's mother when we heard a scream.

"It's coming down!" a voice called, and there was this great, crashing noise. By the time anyone could figure it out, a massive branch from the tree near the book sale cracked off and crashed to the ground.

Right where the book table had been.

Mr. King came running over. "Katie! If we hadn't moved . . ."

I nodded. I couldn't speak. I was crying. Forget Mrs. Luff and her good example.

I suddenly remembered what had happened that day when I was four. Mom and I went to the window to look for the old man who'd been sitting on the steps.

Just then, one of the kids in the neighborhood lost control of his skateboard and came careening so fast into our driveway, he couldn't stop. He smashed into Mom's car and broke his arm.

If it hadn't been the car he hit, it would have been me.

"Mom," I asked. "What did your dad look like?"

She looked surprised. "You know, Katie, you've seen photos of him."

"But those are pictures of him when he was young. What did Grandfather look like right before he died?"

Mom thought for a minute, then smiled.

"Well, he wasn't wearing his teeth," she said. "Too uncomfortable. And he had his favorite old hat on. A stinky old thing he wouldn't let anyone wash."

"Grandfather looked after you really well, didn't he, Mom?"

She squeezed me tight. "Yes. He was a wonderful father."

"Well, he's looking after *me*, now," I said. And I told her the story of how I hadn't gone to the ghost house — the ghost house had come to me.

About the Illustrators

Illustrator of:
The Test
Kelvin Hucker

Kelvin Hucker has been published mainly in educational books and school magazines. Kelvin creates a dark, spooky atmosphere for his illustrations by using a cross-hatching technique.

Illustrator of:
The Worst Thing in the World
The School Fair
Kevin Burgemeestre

Kevin Burgemeestre studied art and design. When Kevin illustrates with ink he uses a dip-in mapping pen in a loose, friendly manner.

The Cover Illustrator
Marc McBride

Marc McBride has illustrated covers for several magazines and children's books. Marc currently creates the realistic images for his covers using acrylic ink with an airbrush. To solve his messy studio problem, he plans to use computer graphics instead.